Truth in Business and Home Lending Discrimination

by

WILBERT SMITH JR.

authorHOUSE®

AuthorHouse™
1663 Liberty Drive, Suite 200
Bloomington, IN 47403
www.authorhouse.com
Phone: 1-800-839-8640

First published by AuthorHouse 12/27/2007

ISBN: 978-1-4343-4798-5 (sc)

Library of Congress Control Number: 2007908892

Printed in the United States of America
Bloomington, Indiana

This book is printed on acid-free paper.

FOREWORD

Friends and colleagues have asked, "What made you decide to write this book?" My answer is, "I have been interested in lending practices for a long time, and have read and heard news about possible discriminations. I decided to research the subject for myself." As I did research, my research did not give me clear answers based on my life experiences. It was very clear that "Discrimination" did exist.

Then I began to think about this: My Dad had served in the Army in World War II and returned home. The GI Bill made it possible for my parents to buy a house, but my Dad was not able to use the GI Bill because the banks would not finance a house for Blacks under the GI Bill nor any other home loan program inside the city. Blacks with very good credit were forced to buy on *Land Contract* with the owner of the older homes, then only inside the *Red Lined Areas*. They were very nice — but old. I realized what prompted me to write this book. The Banks would finance my father a car that cost almost as much as a home, but would not finance a new house.

I feel that if this book helps to clarify these issues, helps to build bridges and not walls, I've met my goals. I want future generations to grow up free of these restrictions — to live in neighborhoods of choice and to prosper. I dedicate this book to my father, Wilbert Smith, Sr.

This study examines the practice of discrimination in bank and government-guaranteed lending in relation to racial and ethnic minorities in the United States. Discrimination in lending is an important issue for society as a whole. The denial of business loans on the basis of the ethnic or racial background of applicants not only denies such individuals the opportunity to establish business enterprises, but such action also retards economic growth in the United States, reduces tax revenues as a consequence, and in many instances increases governmental expenditures for social support services. The denial of residential mortgage loans on the basis of the ethnic or racial background of applicants not only denies such individuals the opportunity to become home owners with all the personal and family benefits that accrue from home ownership, but such action also weakens social stability in the United States, which in turn leads to increased expenditures for police and social services.

Although the existence of statistical disparities between whites and minorities in the extension home mortgage loans is acknowledged by all parties, disagreement exists as to the reasons for these disparities. Equal opportunity activists contend that racial discrimination by mortgage lending institutions is a contributing, if not the primary, source of these patterns. Other parties, however, suggest that the patterns reflect fundamental differences in the economic circumstances of population groups.

To examine and assess the issues stated above, a total of 12 research questions were formulated and investigated. Research questions were investigated in relation to both business loans and residential mortgages. Separate sets of research questions were formulated for the two lending areas. Six research questions were formulated and investigated for each of the two lending areas.

With respect to discrimination in relation to residential mortgage lending, it was concluded that, while HMDA data and studies based on this data provide evidence of disparities between racial and ethnic groups in the approval of home mortgage loans, such evidence does not support conclusively charges of racial discrimination in home mortgage lending. Nevertheless, as a very minimum, these studies indicate a strong potential for and an appearance of the existence of such discrimination.

Becker's theoretical approach to the issue of discrimination in lending against racial minorities appears to be nothing more than an apology for the practice. Becker appears to ignore the facts of the situation. Babbie's conflict theory has some appeal; however, it does not provide a complete explanation. The view of accommodation within the context of the race relations cycle, while not providing a perfect explanation of the practice, does appear to provide a better explanation than either of the other theories.

With respect to discrimination in business lending, a conclusion was drawn that racial and ethnic bias does explain some of the outcomes of SBA lending practices. Racial and ethnic bias, however, was not the only factor involved in different outcomes. Thus, it can be concluded that the SBA is making an honest effort to improve access to financing for minority group applicants.

The findings that the SBA may be making an honest effort in the Los Angeles area to extend business credit in the absence of discriminatory practices, however, must be qualified on two counts. First, the SBA, as an agency of the federal government, may be expected to be more sensitive to racial and ethnic discrimination than are many private sector lenders and than the SBA itself may be under the control of an administration less favorable to minority rights.

Second, the data for the analysis, the results of which were presented in this chapter, was drawn from the Los Angeles metropolitan area. Lending practices in the Los Angeles metropolitan area reasonably may be expected to be more sensitive to racial and ethnic discrimination that may be true in some other areas of the United States, whether the entity approving or extending loans is either affiliated with the federal government or is in the private sector of the economy.

These two qualifications do not compromise the findings of the research. These two qualifications, however, do serve as a caution against an indiscriminate generalization of the findings reported in this chapter to all lending agencies, regardless of geographic location in the United States, and to all private sector lenders in the country.

TABLE OF CONTENTS

LIST OF TABLES

CHAPTER 1:
INTRODUCTION

This research examined the practice of discrimination in bank and government-guaranteed lending in relation to racial and ethnic minorities in the United States. The problem investigated is explained in this chapter, and relevant terms and concepts are defined. The specific research questions addressed are stated, and the methods followed in the investigation of the research questions are described. Lastly, a preview of the remainder of the project is presented in this chapter.

Definitions of Terms

A loan is defined as the extension of funds directly by a lending institution. Operationally, a loan is classified as either approved (money provided) or rejected (money denied).

Discrimination in lending, for purposes of this study, was defined as the determination of the credit worthiness of an individual or business on the basis of factors other than credit history, financial position, earning potential, business experience, loan purpose, or other factors directly relevant to the probability of loan repayment. Personal characteristics such as ethnicity, race, gender, age, and so forth were not considered to be factors directly relevant to the probability of loan repayment.

Racial and ethnic minorities were defined within the context of specific racial and ethnic components of the population in the United States. These population components were as follows: African-American, Asian-American/Pacific Islander, Hispanic-American, and Native American.

Bank was defined as (1) a commercial banking institution that was chartered by either the federal government of the United States or by one of the state governments, (2) a thrift institution——either a savings and loan association or mutual savings bank, or (3) a credit union that was chartered by either the federal government of the United States or by one of the state governments. Government-guaranteed lending was defined as either a business loan or a residential mortgage for which payment to the lender was guaranteed to some extent by an agency of the federal government. With respect to residential mortgages, such agencies included the Federal Housing Authority (FHA) and the Veterans Administration (VA) among others. With respect to business loans, the primary agency considered was the federal-level Small Business Administration (SBA).

An approval rate in the award of loans is defined as the number of approvals divided by the number of applicants. Operationally, an approval rate is expressed as a percentage.

Mean loan amount is defined as the total amount of loans divided by the number of loans extended. Operationally, a mean loan amount is expressed as a dollar value rounded to the nearest $100.

Total loan amount is defined as the total amount of all of the loans extended to a specific population group. Operationally, a total loan amount is expressed as a dollar value rounded to the nearest $1,000.

Problem Statement

Discrimination in lending is an important issue for society as a whole. The denial of business loans on the basis of the ethnic or racial background of applicants not only denies such individuals the opportunity to establish business enterprises, but such action also retards economic growth in the United States, reduces tax revenues as a consequence, and in many instances increases governmental expenditures for social support services. The denial of residential mortgage loans on the basis of the ethnic or racial background of applicants not only denies such individuals the opportunity to become home owners with all the personal and family benefits that accrue from home ownership, but such action also weakens social stability in the United States, which in turn leads to increased expenditures for police and social services.

Since its inception, the SBA has been subject to criticism over the outcome of the agency's lending practices because of perceived inequities between white-owned and minority-owned business firms in the extension of loans.[1] As an example, a State of California Reinvestment Committee found that Hispanic-Americans received only 6.6 percent of the SBA loans granted in that state, although Hispanic-Americans constitute approximately 25 percent of California's population.[2] The SBA makes a valid point when the agency contends that loan percentages should not reflect population proportions; however, such wide gaps as those found by the California Reinvestment Committee invite criticism and demand satisfactory explanation. By vowing to extend more lending to minorities and women, the SBA tacitly admits that the agency's past lending practices have been less than satisfactory.[3]

African-Americans complain the most about being shortchanged by the SBA, pointing out as an example of the problem that the SBA in 1992 awarded only two-percent of the agency's small business loans to African-American applicants.[4] Both white applicants and Asian-American/Pacific Islander applicants tend to receive SBA loans disproportionately high in relation to the population proportions of the two ethnic groups, while African-American, Hispanic-American, and other groups are awarded SBA loans disproportionately low in relation to the population proportions of the groups.[5] This situation has led to a conflict between two minority groups competing for SBA loans. African-American groups contend that Korean-American applicants for SBA loans are given preference over African-American applicants.[6] Korean-American and Japanese-American recipients of SBA loans complain that in the wake of the destruction of their businesses by rioting in predominantly African-American communities, the SBA imposes a requirement that such businesses be rebuilt in the riot-prone communities as a condition of continued SBA financial support.[7] Many Korean-American business owners think that they should receive reparations for riot-related damage to their businesses, as opposed to additional SBA loans.[8]

Bias in lending on the basis of race and ethnic background has an extensive history—both actual and perceived—in the United States. Such bias is charged and investigated most frequently in relation to home mortgages; however, bias in the extension of business loans has also constituted a significant problem in American society over the decades.[9] The SBA has vowed to change the agency's lending practices to provide better access to SBA loans for minority applicants.[10] One such change involves a discontinuance of the SBA's practice of awarding loans on a first-come, first-served basis in favor of focusing loan awards on the basis of community need comparisons. A second change is the implementation of a policy to increase the allocation of funds for loans less than $25,000.[11] Participating lenders are reluctant to extend loans for amounts less than $25,000, although loans in this range are the most in demand by minority applicants for SBA assistance.

Although the existence of statistical disparities between whites and minorities in the extension home mortgage loans is acknowledged by all parties, disagreement exists as to the reasons for these disparities. Equal opportunity activists contend that racial discrimination by mortgage lending institutions "is a contributing, if not the primary, source of these patterns."[12] Other parties, however, "suggest that the patterns reflect fundamental differences in the economic circumstances of population groups."[13]

Research Questions

Research questions were investigated in relation to both business loans and residential mortgages. Separate sets of research questions were formulated for the two lending areas.

With respect to the issue of discrimination in the extension of business loans, six research questions were investigated in this project. These research questions were as follows:

1. Does the approval rate in the award of SBA loans vary between ethnic and racial minority applicants and white (non-Hispanic) applicants?

2. Are there factors other than racial or ethnic bias that explain variation in approval rates in the award of SBA loans to ethnic and racial minority applicants and white (non-Hispanic) applicants?

3. Does the mean loan amount of SBA loans vary between ethnic and racial minority recipients and white (non-Hispanic) recipients?

4. Are there factors other than racial or ethnic bias that explain variation in the mean loan amount of SBA loans to ethnic and racial minority applicants and white (non-Hispanic) applicants?

5. Does the total loan amount of SBA loans vary between ethnic and racial minority recipients and white (non-Hispanic) recipients?

6. Are there factors other than racial or ethnic bias that explain variation in the total loan amount of SBA loans to ethnic and racial minority applicants and white (non-Hispanic) applicants?

With respect to the issue of discrimination in the extension of residential mortgage loans, six research questions were investigated in this project. These research questions were as follows:

7. Does the approval rate in the award of residential mortgage loans vary between ethnic and racial minority applicants and white (non-Hispanic) applicants?

8. Are there factors other than racial or ethnic bias that explain variation in approval rates in the award of residential mortgage loans to ethnic and racial minority applicants and white (non-Hispanic) applicants?

9. Does the mean loan amount of residential mortgage loans vary between ethnic and racial minority recipients and white (non-Hispanic) recipients?

10. Are there factors other than racial or ethnic bias that explain variation in the mean loan amount of residential mortgage

loans to ethnic and racial minority applicants and white (non-Hispanic) applicants?

11. Does the total loan amount of residential mortgage loans vary between ethnic and racial minority recipients and white (non-Hispanic) recipients?

12. Are there factors other than racial or ethnic bias that explain variation in the total loan amount of residential mortgage loans to ethnic and racial minority applicants and white (non-Hispanic) applicants?

Methods

The research design for this project provided for the collection of quantitative data directly relevant to the research questions investigated from governmental agencies. These data then were manipulated to reconstitute them in forms that facilitated the assessment of the data with respect to the research questions investigated. Primarily, such manipulation involved the conversion of absolute data to percentages. In other instances, some data sets were combined to cause the data to conform to the operational definition of ethnic and racial minority used in this research.

Statistical analysis procedures were not employed to determine the probability of statistical significance with respect to discrimination in residential mortgage lending. Rather, percentage distributions were compared in the assessment of the research questions investigated. Statistical analysis procedures were used in the investigation of the research questions pertaining to discrimination in business lending by the SBA. The criteria for assessing the research problems investigated related to residential mortgage lending were as follows:

1. A percentage variance of 10 percent in the approval rate in the award of residential mortgage loans vary between ethnic and racial minority applicants and white (non-Hispanic) applicants was considered to be sufficient evidence for a preliminary finding of the existence of discrimination.

2. The existence of factors other than racial or ethnic bias that explain variation in approval rates in the award of residential mortgage loans to ethnic and racial minority applicants and white (non-Hispanic) applicants to an extent to reduce the overall variation to five-percent or less was considered to be sufficient to negate a finding of the existence of discrimination.

3. A percentage variance of 10 percent in the mean loan amount of residential mortgage loans between ethnic and racial minority recipients and white (non-Hispanic) recipients was considered to be sufficient evidence for a preliminary finding of the existence of discrimination.

4. The existence of factors other than racial or ethnic bias that explain variation in the mean loan amount of residential mortgage loans to ethnic and racial minority applicants and white (non-Hispanic) applicants to an extent to reduce the overall variation to five-percent or less was considered to be sufficient to negate a finding of the existence of discrimination.

5. A percentage variance of 10 percent in the total loan amount of residential mortgage loans between ethnic and racial minority recipients and white (non-Hispanic) recipients was considered to be sufficient evidence for a preliminary finding of the existence of discrimination.

6. The existence of factors other than racial or ethnic bias that explain variation in the total loan amount of residential mortgage loans to ethnic and racial minority applicants and white (non-Hispanic) applicants to an extent to reduce the overall variation to five-percent or less was considered to be sufficient to negate a finding of the existence of discrimination.

Preview of the Remainder of the Project

A review of the literature relevant to the problem investigated is presented in Chapter 2 of the project. The literature review develops a comprehensive development of the problem investigated. The findings of the investigations of the research questions are presented in Chapters 3 and 4 of the project. Chapter 3 is devoted to the findings relevant to discrimination in residential lending, while the findings relevant to discrimination in business lending are presented in Chapter 4. The conclusions drawn from the research findings are presented in Chapter 6.

CHAPTER 2:
REVIEW OF LITERATURE

Literature is reviewed in this chapter that is relevant to the issue of discrimination in bank and government-guaranteed lending in relation to racial and ethnic minorities in the United States. Topical areas covered in this literature review include (1) the general issue of discrimination in lending, (2) bases of discrimination in lending, and (3) the CRA.

The Issue of Discrimination in Lending

Discrimination in bank lending for business purposes is a hotly debated topic.[14] The general contentions of the criticisms of lending practices in relation to businesses is that members of ethnic and racial minority groups, low-income persons, and women are denied access to business credit to greater extents than are white people, middle- and upper income individuals, and men.[15] Most lenders reply that, while the intent of programs to make credit more accessible to all persons is worthy, the implementation of the programs fail to recognize the realities of the financial marketplace.[16]

The relationship between discrimination in bank lending for business purposes and discrimination in lending generally is interlocking to the extent that an assessment of one aspect of discrimination in lending cannot proceed effectively without addressing the other half of the discrimination in lending equation.[17] Further, any investigation of discrimination in lending based on socioeconomic status cannot be divorced from discrimination based on ethnicity, race, and gender because of the strong ties among the four variables in relation to accessibility to credit.[18]

Discrimination in the extension of credit is volatile issue in the United States.[19] Although federal government efforts to end such discrimination have been pursued for two decades, critics contend that much work is still required.[20]

Discrimination in lending is a part of the larger problem of housing discrimination.[21] Discrimination exists in the United States with respect to a variety of factors. The most publicized form of discrimination is that associated with racial and ethnic background. Such discrimination is also based at times on age, sexual preference, behavior, and other factors. The means by which discrimination is applied to lending vary. Overt refusal to lend money to an individual because of racial or ethnic background is not only illegal in the United States, it is also relatively rare. Such legal prohibitions are often circumvented in a number of ways, however, such as a failure to offer certain loan programs to certain individuals, and rejection on the basis of other factors that appear unrelated to racial or ethnic background, but which, in fact, may be contrived, and may not be applied equally to white applicants.[22] Although illegal, this practice often results in the denial of funds to members of racial and ethnic minorities, and even to neighborhoods that are predominantly occupied by members of racial and ethnic minorities.[23] This latter practice is known as "redlining."

In 1977, the CRA became law.[24] The CRA deals with two of the specific issues of overriding interest in the equal opportunity area—

equal access to housing, and equal access to credit. The CRA was, in 1977, the latest in a series of federal laws designed to attack the problems of unequal access to credit that were confronting some segments of the American population. The CRA was related to these other laws, but the act and its provisions were specifically designed to deal with the problems related to mortgage and business lending, to establish guidelines for bankers, and to provide a mechanism for public review and protest. Public concerns related to equal opportunity in housing and credit ranged from the ability of some groups to obtain housing and credit in certain areas to the ability of members of many of these same groups to obtain financing for either housing or business in areas where it was accessible to them. This type of loan policy or practice constituted open discrimination, and, as such, was somewhat more easily dealt with on a legal plane, if not in actual practice than were some other forms of discrimination.

The CRA, therefore, is a component of that group of equal opportunity legislation that addresses problems related to housing and credit.[25] The first of the laws comprising this component of the equal opportunity legislation was the *Fair Housing Act*, which was actually Title VIII of the *Civil Rights Act* enacted in 1968. The *Fair Housing Act* is an open housing law that prohibits discrimination on the basis of race, color, religion, or national origin. This act was intended to halt the practice of denying access to housing (either purchase or rental) on the basis of personal characteristics. In 1974, the discrimination provisions were expanded to prohibit the denial of access to housing on the basis of an individual's sex, and the denial of access provisions were expanded to housing-related credit extensions. These expansions of the equal housing opportunity legislation were implemented via the *Community Development Act*. Prohibitions against discrimination in housing and credit extension on the basis of age and handicap were enacted in 1988, as a part of the bill to extend the *Civil Rights Act*.

Official concern with credit extension was expanded again in 1975, with the enactment of the *Home Mortgage Disclosure Act*.[26] This act made it a less difficult for both individuals and public officials to ascertain whether depository institutions were in fact discriminating in the granting of credit. The *Home Mortgage Disclosure Act* (HMDA) was structured to deal with discrimination on the basis of geographic criteria, and was perceived as a means of dealing with the problem of redlining. Thus, the geographic criteria were conceived of as indirect means of attacking discrimination in credit against minority population groups that were restricted to living within specific sections of urban areas.

The CRA, the *Fair Housing Act*, the *Community Development Act*, and the HMDA should have eliminated discrimination from financing.[27] That charges of the existence of such discrimination persist in the 1990s is evidence either that the legislation has not been effectively enforced, or the problem is misunderstood by some parties.

The premise upon which the CRA is based was a Congressional finding that banks and thrifts have a continuing and affirmative obligation to help meet the credit needs of the local communities in which they are chartered.[28] This finding stemmed from the view that, as society represented by government has granted these institutions special privileges (charters to do business, deposit insurance, and access to the Federal Reserve discount window), these institutions have an obligation to serve the public, particularly that segment of the public in the communities in which the institutions are chartered. The CRA, thus, was intended to encourage lenders to continually communicate with the members of their local communities about the credit needs of the community, and to help the members of their local communities to meet those local credit needs—particularly where low- and moderate-income neighborhoods were concerned.

Bases of Discrimination in Lending

The most consistent of the criticisms against lenders in the mid-1970s concerned the practice of redlining—the denial of credit within specifically defined geographical areas.[29] In actual practice, redlined areas were almost always those in which high concentrations of minority population groups resided. The equal housing legislation enacted prior to the CRA focused on the individual applicant, barring, in most instances, consideration of personal characteristics in determining creditworthiness. At this point, Congress turned its attention to what were considered to be the arbitrary consideration of geographic factors in determining creditworthiness. Congress determined that lenders had, at times, contributed to the decline of certain neighborhoods by their failure to provide financing to qualified applicants in those areas.

Another serious charge laid against lenders was that they accumulated deposits from the residents of redlined areas and from members of minority population groups, and then refused to extend credit to such residents or minority group members, who were, more often than not, one and the same.[30] The CRA was designed, in part, to assure that credit would be extended to those from whom lending institutions accepted deposits, assuming that such individuals were otherwise eligible for such credit.

Analyses of HMDA data for 1987 found that mortgage lending institutions in both Atlanta and Detroit "extended roughly three to four times more home purchase loans per single family housing unit in the predominantly white neighborhoods than in the predominantly minority areas."[31] Similar analyses conducted a year later produced similar results for Chicago, Denver, Louisville, Minneapolis, and

Washington, D.C. Although the existence of statistical disparities between whites and minorities in the extension home mortgage loans is acknowledged by all parties, disagreement exists as to the reasons for these disparities. Equal opportunity activists contend that racial discrimination by mortgage lending institutions "is a contributing, if not the primary, source of these patterns."[32] Other parties "suggest that the patterns reflect fundamental differences in the economic circumstances of population groups."[33]

Some observers suggest that discrimination in lending against racial minorities may be explained by the stage of accommodation in the race relations cycle.[34] Applying this theory would suggest that credit becomes more accessible for members of minority groups as the members of such groups adopt more of the characteristics of the population majority. This theory tends to explain both why a growing African-American middle-class finds bank credit increasingly more accessible, and why the majority of African-Americans continue to find bank credit exceedingly difficult to obtain.

By contrast, economist Gary Becker uses the economic theory of discrimination to contend that the fact that African-Americans receive disproportionately less bank credit than do white Americans is not in fact discrimination.[35] Becker contends that firms can afford to discriminate only if they are in a monopsony situation or if all competitors in their region also practice discrimination.[36] In the latter context, it is also necessary for the competitors to have, essentially, the same taste for discrimination; that is, all must be willing to pay the same price to be able to discriminate.

Becker does not think that the HMDA data necessarily provide evidence of discrimination in mortgage lending.[37] Becker bases his contention on his theory of discrimination in the market place.[38] This theory demands that discriminators sacrifice profits in order to discriminate against a particular population group. First, Becker contends that the HMDA data provide no basis for making such an assessment because default rates, late payments, interest rates, and other determinants of profitability for various racial and ethnic groups are not measured.[39] Second, if discrimination in mortgage lending were occurring, mortgage bankers would lend to only the most credit worthy minority applicants, thereby causing minority mortgage lending to be more profitable than mortgage lending to whites. The study of mortgage lending in the Boston metropolitan area conducted by the Federal Reserve Bank of Boston where default rates were collected, however, found no difference in default rates between whites and minority applicants approved for home loans. Thus, mortgage lenders in the Boston area do not appear to be seeking only the most credit worthy minority applicants, while accepting less qualified white applicants. Becker also points out that minority-owned banks and other institutions specializing in loans to minority groups "have not tended to be particularly profitable," and that this fact tends to support the contention that factors affecting profitability, rather than racial discrimination explain differences among minority groups in relation to home loan approval rates.[40]

Another explanation for the practice of discrimination in lending against racial minorities may be found in class conflict theory.[41] The conflict paradigm describes social life as a struggle among competing individuals and groups. The Marxist interpretation of the conflict paradigm is made within the concept of class struggle. Conflict theory views such discrimination within the context of dominant population groups acting as the owners or at least the possessors of a valuable societal resource who are unwilling to share that resource with other societal classes or population groups.

The CRA

The CRA may be considered to be the first law to set standards of social responsibility for the banking industry. The CRA provides for assessments in connection with examinations and rewards and sanctions in connection with applications for the creation and expansion of banks and savings institutions.[42]

Additionally, the CRA was designed to provide guidance as to how regulatory agencies would assess the records of mortgage lenders in the satisfaction of their continuing and affirmative obligations to help meet the credit needs of their local communities, while continuing to fulfill the conditions of safe and sound financial operations.

The CRA was also motivated by a distrust in Congress of the willingness of executive departments, specifically, the Departments of Housing and Urban Development and Justice, to aggressively enforce the provisions of the Fair Housing Act.[43] The most consistent of the criticisms against lenders in the mid-1970s concerned the practice of redlining—the denial of credit within specifically defined geographical areas. In actual practice, redlined areas were almost always those in which high concentrations of minority population groups resided. The equal housing legislation enacted prior to the CRA focused on the individual applicant, barring, in most instances, consideration of personal characteristics in determining creditworthiness. At this point, Congress turned its attention to what were considered to be the arbitrary consideration of geographic factors in determining creditworthiness. Congress determined that lenders had, at times, contributed to the decline of certain neighborhoods by their failure to provide financing to qualified applicants in those areas.

CHAPTER 3:
DISCRIMINATION IN RESIDENTIAL LENDING

Data and analyses are presented in this chapter with respect to discrimination in residential lending. The key factor that should dissuade a lender from discriminating in residential lending is the CRA, which was discussed briefly in the preceding chapter. Greater detail on the requirements of the CRA are presented in this chapter. These requirements are followed by an assessment of residential lending practices.

CRA Requirements

The CRA requires the regulating agencies to take into account an institution's record in meeting its community's credit needs, when evaluating applications for either the creation or the relocation of domestic branch offices or for merger with or acquisition of another institution.[44] The requirements imposed on lending institutions to facilitate the evaluation of an institution's record in meeting the credit obligations of its community include the following elements:[45]

1. A description of the institution's community. Such community description may be based on existing political boundaries, its effective lending territory, or any other reasonably described local area that fulfills the purpose of the CRA and that does not unreasonably exclude low- and moderate-income neighborhoods. Further, a bank may describe a single community or a number of local communities that, together, make up its entire community.

2. Adoption of a CRA statement for each of the separate community descriptions effected by the lending institution. Mandatory components in such statements are (a) a map of the community described, (b) a listing of the specific types of credit the institution is prepared to extend within the community, and (c) a copy of the public notice concerning the CRA.

3. Institutions must maintain files of all comments received from the public that specifically relate to any of the institution's CRA statements or to the record of the institution in meeting the credit needs of its community or communities.

The CRA includes other actions that lenders are encouraged to take.[46] These actions as follows:

1. A lender is urged to describe how its current efforts help to meet the credit needs of its local community or communities.

2. A lender is encouraged to issue periodic reports assessing the institution's efforts in meeting the credit needs of its local community or communities.

3. A lender is encouraged to describe institutional efforts to ascertain the credit needs of its local community or communities.

There are fourteen specific assessment factors that are employed by the regulatory agencies in the evaluation of an institution's.[47] These assessment factors are as follows:

1. The first basis for assessment covers those activities conducted by the bank to ascertain the credit needs of its community. These factors include the extent of the bank's efforts to communicate with members of the community regarding the credit services offered by the bank to residents of the community.

2. The second basis for assessment is the extent of the bank's marketing and special credit-related programs to make members of the community aware to the credit services offered by the bank.

3. The third basis for assessment is the extent of participation by the bank's board of directors in formulating the bank's policies and reviewing its performance with respect to the purposes of the CRA.

4. The fourth basis for assessment covers any practices by the institution that appear to be intended to discourage applications for types of credit set forth in the institution's CRA statement or statements.

5. The fifth basis for assessment is the geographic distribution of the bank's credit extensions, credit applications, and credit denials.

6. The sixth basis for assessment is any evidence of prohibited discriminatory or other illegal credit practices.

7. The seventh basis for assessment is an institution's record of opening or closing offices in minority neighborhoods and in providing services at offices.

8. The eighth basis for assessment is an institution's participation, including investments, in local community development and redevelopment projects or programs.

9. The ninth basis for assessment is an institution's origination of residential mortgage loans, housing rehabilitation loans, home improvement loans, and small business or small farm loans within its community, or the purchase of those loans originated in the community.

10. The tenth basis for assessment is an institution's participation in governmentally insured, guaranteed, or subsidized loan programs for housing, small businesses, or small farms.

11. The eleventh basis for assessment is an institution's ability to meet various community credit needs based on its financial condition, size, legal impediments, local economic conditions, and other factors.

12. The twelfth basis for assessment covers any other factors that, in an agency's judgment, reasonably bear upon the extent to which an institution is helping to meet the credit needs of its entire community.

13. The thirteenth basis for assessment is an institution's CRA statement (or statements) and other signed comments retained by the institution.

14. The fourteenth basis for assessment is an institution's performance in helping to meet the credit needs of the

institution's entire community, including low- and moderate-income neighborhoods, as such performance remains consistent with safe and sound operational practices.

Assessment of Recent Mortgage Lending Practices

As stated in the preceding chapter, analyses of HMDA data for 1987 found that mortgage lending institutions in both Atlanta and Detroit "extended roughly three to four times more home purchase loans per single family housing unit in the predominantly white neighborhoods than in the predominantly minority areas."[48] As also stated, similar analyses conducted a year later produced similar results for Chicago, Denver, Louisville, Minneapolis, and Washington, D.C.[49]

Although the existence of statistical disparities between whites and minorities in the extension home mortgage loans is acknowledged by all parties, disagreement exists as to the reasons for these disparities. As stated in the preceding chapter, equal opportunity activists contend that racial discrimination by mortgage lending institutions "is a contributing, if not the primary, source of these patterns."[50] Other parties "suggest that the patterns reflect fundamental differences in the economic circumstances of population groups."[51]

To test the competing explanations, HMDA data for 1990 and 1991 are summarized and compared. HMDA data for 1990 are summarized in Tables 1 through 4. The data presented in Tables 1 and 2 summarize the disposition of home loan applications by racial and ethnic group for government-backed mortgages (Table 1) and conventional mortgages (Table 2). The tables may be found on page 27 (Table 1) and page 28 (Table 2).

The data presented in both Tables 1 and 2 reflect higher approval rates for whites and Asian/Pacific Islanders than for other racial and ethnic groups, and substantially lower approval rates for African Americans than for any other racial or ethnic group. The lower approval rates for African American applicants are even more pronounced in relation to conventional mortgages than in relation to government-backed mortgages.

The data presented in Tables 3 and 4 summarize the approval rates for home loan applicants when controlled for both racial and ethnic group and for applicant income for both government-backed mortgages (Table 3) and conventional mortgages (Table 4). The tables may be found on page 29 (Table 3) and page 30 (Table 4). Generally, the data reflect rising approval rates for all racial and ethnic groups as applicant income rises, with some exceptions at the highest income level. Regardless of income level, however, whites and Asians/Pacific Islanders are approved more frequently than are other racial and ethnic groups, and African Americans are approved less frequently than any other racial or ethnic group. Again, these patterns are even more pronounced in relation to conventional mortgages than in relation to government-backed mortgages. Approval rates tend to rise more rapidly from the lowest income group to the higher income groups for other racial and ethnic groups than is true for African American applicants.

HMDA data for 1991 are summarized in Tables 5 through 8. The data presented in Tables 5 and 6 summarize the disposition of home loan applications by racial and ethnic group for government-backed mortgages (Table 5) and conventional mortgages (Table 6). The tables may be found on page 31 (Table 5) and page 32 (Table 6). The most recent economic recession in the United States began in 1990 and became more entrenched in 1991. Therefore, one would anticipate lower home loan approval rates in 1991 than in 1990. This outcome prevailed in relation to conventional mortgages. In relation to government-backed mortgages, however, approval rates were lower for white applicants but higher for minority applicants.

The home loan approval patterns in 1991, however, remained similar to those for 1990. Whites and Asians/Pacific Islanders were approved more frequently than other racial and ethnic groups, while African Americans were approved less frequently.

The data presented in Tables 7 and 8 summarize the approval rates for home loan applicants when controlled for both racial and ethnic group and for applicant income for both government-backed mortgages (Table 7) and conventional mortgages (Table 8). The tables may be found on page 33 (Table 7) and page 34 (Table 8). Generally, as was true in 1990, the data reflect rising approval rates for all racial and ethnic groups as applicant income rises, with some exceptions at the highest income level. Regardless of income level, however, whites and Asians/Pacific Islanders continued to be approved more frequently than are other racial and ethnic groups, and African Americans are approved less frequently than any other racial or ethnic group. Again, these patterns are even more pronounced in relation to conventional mortgages than in relation to government-backed mortgages. Again, following the patterns of 1990, approval rates tend to rise more rapidly from the lowest income group to the higher income groups for other racial and ethnic groups than is true for African American applicants.

Chapter Conclusion

While HMDA data and studies based on this data provide evidence of disparities between racial and ethnic groups in the approval of home mortgage loans, such evidence does not support conclusively charges of racial discrimination in home mortgage lending. Nevertheless, as a very minimum, these studies indicate a strong potential for and an appearance of the existence of such discrimination.

Becker's theoretical approach to the issue of discrimination in lending against racial minorities appears to be nothing more than an apology for the practice. Becker appears to ignore the facts of the situation. Babbie's conflict theory has some appeal; however, it does not provide a complete explanation. The view of accommodation within the context of the race relations cycle, while not providing a perfect explanation of the practice, does appear to provide a better explanation than either of the other theories.

TABLE 1

Disposition of Home Loan Applications by Racial and Ethnic Background: Government-Backed Mortgages 1990

Racial/Ethnic Group	Disposition of Applications (%)				
	Approved	Denied	Withdrawn File	Closed	Total
African American	60.9	26.3	11.3	1.5	100
American Indian/ Alaskan Native	63.5	22.5	12.8	1.2	100
Asian/Pacific Islander	74.8	12.8	11.6	.8	100
Hispanic	68.7	18.4	11.6	1.3	100
White	77.4	12.1	9.7	.8	100
Other	66.3	18.4	13.8	1.5	100
Joint (white/minority)	75.6	14.1	9.5	.8	100

[Source: Canner, Smith, Bowen, Benkovic, Freeland, Johnson, Orndorff, and Schultz, 1991]

TABLE 2

Disposition of Home Loan Applications by Racial and Ethnic Background: Conventional Mortgages 1990

Racial/Ethnic Group	Disposition of Applications (%)				
	Approved	Denied	Withdrawn File	Closed	Total
African American	55.7	33.9	9.4	1.0	100
American Indian/ Alaskan Native	66.0	22.4	10.6	1.0	100
Asian/Pacific Islander	72.7	12.9	13.5	.9	100
Hispanic	65.1	21.4	12.4	1.1	100
White	75.5	14.4	9.4	.7	100
Other	68.2	19.0	11.9	.9	100
Joint (white/minority)	78.3	14.9	11.1	.7	100

[Source: Canner, Smith, Bowen, Benkovic, Freeland, Johnson, Orndorff, and Schultz, 1991]

TABLE 3

Home Loan Approvals by Racial and Ethnic Background, and
Applicant Income: Government-Backed Mortgages 1990

Racial/Ethnic Group	Income As A Percent of Metro Area Average			
	Less Than 80	80-99	100-120	More Than 120
African American	58.5	64.5	65.7	68.0
American Indian/ Alaskan Native	63.5	70.2	68.0	71.3
Asian/Pacific Islander	75.0	78.4	78.1	76.0
Hispanic	66.5	72.2	73.9	72.4
White	76.5	81.0	81.9	82.4
Other	67.7	72.0	69.6	67.3
Joint (white/minority)	74.1	78.2	77.6	79.2

[Source: Canner, Smith, Bowen, Benkovic, Freeland, Johnson, Orndorff, and Schultz, 1991]

29

TABLE 4

Home Loan Approvals by Racial and Ethnic Background, and
Applicant Income: Conventional Mortgages 1990

Racial/Ethnic Group	Income As A Percent of Metro Area Average			
	Less Than 80	80-99	100-120	More Than 120
African American	51.4	60.8	63.8	65.7
American Indian/ Alaskan Native	62.7	73.3	72.6	74.4
Asian/Pacific Islander	68.4	75.1	75.0	75.2
Hispanic	58.1	67.7	69.6	71.1
White	69.0	78.1	80.4	81.2
Other	64.5	70.6	72.1	71.0
Joint (white/ minority)	64.8	72.2	75.8	77.6

[Source: Canner, Smith, Bowen, Benkovic, Freeland, Johnson, Orndorff, and Schultz, 1991]

TABLE 5

Disposition of Home Loan Applications by Racial and Ethnic Background: Government-Backed Mortgages 1991

Racial/Ethnic Group	Disposition of Applications (%)				
	Approved	Denied	Withdrawn File	Closed	Total
African American	61.4	26.4	10.3	1.9	100
American Indian/ Alaskan Native	64.2	22.1	12.1	1.6	100
Asian/Pacific Islander	74.9	12.5	11.4	1.2	100
Hispanic	68.4	18.9	11.0	1.7	100
White	74.3	16.3	8.3	1.1	100
Other	68.7	16.3	12.6	2.4	100
Joint (white/minority)	74.0	15.9	9.1	1.0	100

[Source: Canner and Smith, 1992]

TABLE 6

Disposition of Home Loan Applications by Racial and Ethnic Background: Conventional Mortgages 1991

Racial/Ethnic Group	**Disposition of Applications (%)**				
	Approved	Denied	Withdrawn File	Closed	Total
African American	53.3	37.6	8.0	1.1	100
American Indian/ Alaskan Native	62.4	27.3	8.8	1.5	100
Asian/Pacific Islander	72.6	15.0	11.0	1.4	100
Hispanic	61.5	26.6	10.3	1.6	100
White	73.7	17.3	8.2	.8	100
Other	67.2	19.9	11.5	1.4	100
Joint (white/minority)	71.9	17.5	9.8	.8	100

[Source: Canner and Smith, 1992]

TABLE 7

Home Loan Approvals by Racial and Ethnic Background, and
Applicant Income: Government-Backed Mortgages 1991

Racial/Ethnic Group	Income As A Percent of Metro Area Average			
	Less Than 80	80-99	100-120	More Than 120
African American	58.8	66.8	66.9	69.3
American Indian/ Alaskan Native	61.0	68.5	71.2	69.8
Asian/Pacific Islander	72.3	78.8	78.7	78.3
Hispanic	64.6	70.8	71.2	75.7
White	67.3	79.5	81.0	81.8
Other	68.9	69.4	75.9	73.2
Joint (white/minority)	67.1	76.4	79.1	79.2

[Source: Canner and Smith, 1992]

TABLE 8

Home Loan Approvals by Racial and Ethnic Background, and
Applicant Income: Conventional Mortgages 1991

Racial/Ethnic Group	Income As A Percent of Metro Area Average			
	Less Than 80	80-99	100-120	More Than 120
African American	44.9	60.7	63.9	66.0
American Indian/ Alaskan Native	53.9	69.4	73.9	73.4
Asian/Pacific Islander	68.5	75.1	75.5	74.3
Hispanic	54.0	64.9	67.0	68.5
White	61.7	77.0	79.9	81.0
Other	63.0	69.7	70.1	70.4
Joint (white/minority)	59.2	72.9	75.0	76.8

[Source: Canner and Smith, 1992]

CHAPTER 4:
DISCRIMINATION IN
BUSINESS LENDING

Discrimination in business lending was investigated within the context of the lending practices of the United States Small Business Administration (SBA). The SBA functions under the cabinet-level supervision of the Secretary of Commerce, and both provides direct loans and participates (through guarantees) in intermediate loans to small business firms to finance plant and facilities construction, the acquisition of machinery and equipment, process conversion, and expansion. The SBA also provides to small business firms a variety of counseling and managerial assistance programs.

Background on the Issue

The SBA functions under the cabinet-level supervision of the Secretary of Commerce, and both provides direct loans and participates (through guarantees) in intermediate loans to small business firms to finance plant and facilities construction, the acquisition of machinery and equipment, process conversion, and expansion. The SBA also provides to small business firms a variety of counseling and managerial assistance programs.

Since its inception, the SBA has been subject to criticism over the outcome of the agency's lending practices because of perceived inequities between white-owned and minority-owned business firms in the extension of loans.[52] As an example, a California Reinvestment Committee found that Hispanics received only 6.6 percent of the SBA loans granted in that state, although Hispanics constitute approximately 25 percent of California's population.[53] The SBA makes a valid point when the agency contends that loan percentages should not reflect population proportions; however, such wide gaps as those found by the California Reinvestment Committee invite criticism and demand satisfactory explanation. By vowing to extend more lending to minorities and women, the SBA tacitly admits that the agency's past lending practices have been less than satisfactory.[54]

African-Americans complain the most about being shortchanged by the SBA, pointing out as an example of the problem that the SBA in 1992 awarded only two-percent of the agency's small business loans to African-American applicants.[55] Both white applicants and Asian-American applicants tend to receive SBA loans disproportionately high in relation to the population proportions of the two ethnic groups, while African-American, Hispanic, and other groups are awarded SBA loans disproportionately low in relation to the population proportions of the groups.[56] This situation has led to a conflict between two minority groups competing for SBA loans. African-American groups contend that Korean-American applicants for SBA loans are given preference over African- American applicants.[57] Korean-American and Japanese-American recipients of SBA loans complain that in the wake of the destruction of their businesses by rioting in predominantly African-American communities, the SBA imposes a requirement that such businesses be rebuilt in the riot-prone communities as a condition of continued SBA financial support.[58] Many Korean-American business owners think that they should receive reparations for riot-related damage to their businesses, as opposed to additional SBA loans.[59]

Bias in lending on the basis of race and ethnic background has an extensive history—both actual and perceived—in the United States. Such bias is charged and investigated most frequently in relation to home mortgages; however, bias in the extension of business loans has also constituted a significant problem in American society over the decades.[60] The SBA has vowed to change the agency's lending practices to provide better access to SBA loans for minority applicants.[61] One such change involves a discontinuance of the SBA's practice of awarding loans on a first-come, first-served basis in favor of focusing loan awards on the basis of community need comparisons. A second change is the implementation of a policy to increase the allocation of funds for loans less than $25,000.[62] Participating lenders are reluctant to extend loans for amounts less than $25,000, although loans in this range are the most in demand by minority applicants for SBA assistance. The SBA tends to be hampered in the Agencies efforts to aid low-income persons by prevailing political imperatives.

Investigatory Approach

Six research questions were investigated to assess the performance of the SBA with respect to discrimination in business lending. These research questions were as follows:

1. Does the approval rate in the award of SBA loans vary between ethnic and racial minority applicants and white (non-Hispanic) applicants?

2. Are there factors other than racial or ethnic bias that explain variation in approval rates in the award of SBA loans to ethnic

and racial minority applicants and white (non-Hispanic) applicants?

3. Does the mean loan amount of SBA loans vary between ethnic and racial minority recipients and white (non-Hispanic) recipients?

4. Are there factors other than racial or ethnic bias that explain variation in the mean loan amount of SBA loans to ethnic and racial minority applicants and white (non-Hispanic) applicants?

5. Does the total loan amount of SBA loans vary between ethnic and racial minority recipients and white (non-Hispanic) recipients?

6. Are there factors other than racial or ethnic bias that explain variation in the total loan amount of SBA loans to ethnic and racial minority applicants and white (non-Hispanic) applicants?

The dependent variable in the analysis of research question number one is the approval rate in the award of SBA loans. The independent variable is population group classification.

The dependent variables in the analysis of research question number two are applicant prior business experience, applicant financial position, applicant prior credit history, and the potential business viability of the underlying purpose of a loan. The independent variable is population group classification.

The dependent variable in the analysis of research question number three is the mean loan amount of SBA loans awarded. The independent variable is population group classification.

The dependent variables in the analysis of research question number four are applicant prior business experience, applicant financial position, applicant prior credit history, and the potential business viability of the underlying purpose of a loan. The independent variable is population group classification.

The dependent variable in the analysis of research question number five is the total loan amount of SBA loans awarded. The independent variable is population group classification.

The dependent variables in the analysis of research question number six are applicant prior business experience, applicant financial position, applicant prior credit history, and the potential business viability of the underlying purpose of a loan. The independent variable is population group classification.

An SBA loan in this study was defined as either a loan extended directly by the agency or a participating loan in which the SBA acted as a guarantor. Operationally, an SBA loan was classified as either approved (money provided) or rejected (money denied).

Race and ethnic background were defined in this study as the declaration of a subject. Thus, a subject stating that he or she is an African-American was classified as an African-American. Operationally, the race or ethnic background of a subject was classified in this study as either African-American or Korean-American.

An approval rate in the award of SBA loans was defined in this study as the number of approvals divided by the number of applicants. Operationally, an approval rate was expressed in this study as a percentage.

Mean loan amount was defined in this study as the total amount of loans divided by the number of loans extended. Operationally, a mean loan amount was expressed in this study as a dollar value rounded to the nearest $100.

Total loan amount was defined in this study as the total amount of all of the SBA loans extended to a specific population group.

Operationally, a total loan amount was expressed in this study as a dollar value rounded to the nearest $1,000.

Factors other than racial or ethnic bias were defined in this study as an applicant's prior business experience, an applicant's financial position, an applicant's prior credit history, and the potential business viability of the underlying purpose of the loan. Operationally, an applicant's prior business experience, financial position, prior credit history, and the potential business viability of the underlying purpose of a loan were all expressed as "strong," "moderate," or "weak." Classifications for subjects in relation to these factors were based on declarations by the individual subjects.

The term statistical significance as used in this study refers to the mathematical probability that a quantitative outcome of data analysis represents a real difference as opposed to a mathematical accident. Racial or ethnic bias as used in this study indicated a statistically significant difference in the treatment of different population groups in the absence of differences in other factors to explain such an outcome.

Data pertaining to business owners in the Watts and Koreatown sections of Los Angeles were obtained to develop the data required for this study. These data were subjected to statistical analysis in the investigation of the research questions formulated for this study.

The research questions were analyzed through the application of analysis of variance (ANOVA) procedures to the appropriate data. ANOVAs were performed in relation to each of the research questions analyzed. Statistical significance was established at the $p<.05$ level of probability.

Research Results and Findings

Research questions one and two were concerned with SBA loan approval rates. Research questions three and four were concerned with mean loan amounts of SBA loans. Research questions five and six were concerned with total loan amounts of SBA loans by population groups. The findings of the tests of the hypotheses are presented in the discussions that follow.

SBA Loan Approval Rates

SBA loan approval rates were found to be higher for white applicants (37.2 percent) than for African-American applicants (24.8 percent). The difference in loan approval rates between the two population groups was statistically significant ($F=4.571$, $df=1,102$, $p<.05$). Thus research question number one was answered in the affirmative.

Differences between white applicants and African-American applicants for SBA loans were found to be statistically significant in relation to both applicant financial position ($F=4.124$, $df=2,101$, $p<.05$) and applicant prior credit history ($F=6.055$, $df=2,101$, $p<.05$). Thus research question number two was answered in the affirmative.

SBA Loan Amount Means

The mean SBA loan amounts were found to be higher for white loan recipients ($157,200) than for African-American loan recipients ($131,400). The difference in mean loan amounts between the two population groups was statistically significant ($F=5.462$, $df=1,102$, $p<.05$). Thus research question number three was answered in the affirmative.

Differences between white loan recipients and African-American loan recipients of SBA loans were not found to be statistically significant in relation to applicant business experience, applicant financial position, applicant prior credit history, or the potential business viability of the underlying purpose of the loan. Thus research question number four was answered in the negative.

SBA Loan Amount Totals

The total SBA loan amounts were found to be higher for white loan recipients ($2.7 million) than for African-American loan recipients ($1.9 million). Thus research question number five was answered in the affirmative.

This difference was a result of the combination of a higher loan approval rate for white applicants (explainable by factors other than racial or ethnic bias) and a higher mean loan amount for white loan recipients (not explainable by factors other than racial or ethnic bias). Thus research question number six was answered partially in the affirmative and partially in the negative. To the extent that the difference in total loan amounts may be attributed to loan approval rates, the difference may not be considered to be due to racial or ethnic bias. To the extent that the difference in total loan amounts may be attributed to mean loan amounts, however, the difference may be considered to be due to racial or ethnic bias. Approximately 50.7 percent of the difference in total loan amounts was attributable to differences in loan approval rates, while approximately 49.3 percent of the difference in total loan amounts was attributable to differences in mean loan amounts. Thus approximately one-half of the difference in total loan amounts may be said to be due to racial or ethnic bias.

Chapter Conclusion

Based on the findings of the research performed for this current study, a conclusion was drawn that racial and ethnic bias does explain some of the outcomes of SBA lending practices. Racial and ethnic bias, however, was not the only factor involved in different outcomes. Thus, it can be concluded that the SBA is making an honest effort to improve access to financing for minority group applicants.

The findings that the SBA may be making an honest effort in the Los Angeles area to extend business credit in the absence of discriminatory practices, however, must be qualified on two counts. First, the SBA, as an agency of the federal government may be expected to be more sensitive to racial and ethnic discrimination than are many private sector lenders and than the SBA itself may be under the control of an administration less favorable to minority rights.

Second, the data for the analysis, the results of which were presented in this chapter, was drawn from the Los Angeles metropolitan area. Lending practices in the Los Angeles metropolitan area reasonably may be expected to be more sensitive to racial and ethnic discrimination that may be true in some other areas of the United States, whether the entity approving or extending loans is either affiliated with the federal government or is in the private sector of the economy.

These two qualifications do not compromise the findings of the research reported in this chapter. These two qualifications, however, do serve as a caution against an indiscriminate generalization of the findings reported in this chapter to all lending agencies, regardless of geographic location in the United States, and to all private sector lenders in the country.

CHAPTER 5:
SUBPRIME LENDING AND DISCRIMINATION

This study examined the practice of discrimination in bank and government-guaranteed lending in relation to racial and ethnic minorities in the United States. Discrimination in lending is an important issue for society as a whole. The denial of business loans on the basis of the ethnic or racial background of applicants not only denies such individuals the opportunity to establish business enterprises, but such action also retards economic growth in the United States, reduces tax revenues as a consequence, and in many instances increases governmental expenditures for social support services. The denial of residential mortgage loans on the basis of the ethnic or racial background of applicants not only denies such individuals the opportunity to become home owners with all the personal and family benefits that accrue from home ownership, but such action also weakens social stability in the United States, which in turn leads to increased expenditures for police and social services.

Since its inception, the SBA has been subject to criticism over the outcome of the agency's lending practices because of perceived inequities between white-owned and minority-owned business firms in the extension of loans. As an example, a State of California Reinvestment Committee found that Hispanic-Americans received only 6.6 percent of the SBA loans granted in that state, although Hispanic-Americans constitute approximately 25 percent of California's population. The SBA makes a valid point when the agency contends that loan percentages should not reflect population proportions; however, such wide gaps as those found by the California Reinvestment Committee invite criticism and demand satisfactory explanation. By vowing to extend more lending to minorities and women, the SBA tacitly admits that the agency's past lending practices have been less than satisfactory.

Bias in lending on the basis of race and ethnic background has an extensive history—both actual and perceived—in the United States. Such bias is charged and investigated most frequently in relation to home mortgages; however, bias in the extension of business loans has also constituted a significant problem in American society over the decades. Under the Clinton Administration, the SBA has vowed to change the agency's lending practices to provide better access to SBA loans for minority applicants. One such change involves a discontinuance of the SBA's practice of awarding loans on a first-come, first-served basis in favor of focusing loan awards on the basis of community need comparisons. A second change is the implementation of a policy to increase the allocation of funds for loans less than $25,000. Participating lenders are reluctant to extend loans for amounts less than $25,000, although loans in this range are the most in demand by minority applicants for SBA assistance.

Although the existence of statistical disparities between whites and minorities in the extension home mortgage loans is acknowledged by all parties, disagreement exists as to the reasons for these disparities. Equal opportunity activists contend that racial discrimination by mortgage lending institutions is a contributing, if not the primary, source of these patterns. Other parties, however, suggest that the patterns reflect fundamental differences in the economic circumstances of population groups.

To examine and assess the issues stated above, a total of 12 research questions were formulated and investigated. Research questions were investigated in relation to both business loans and residential mortgages. Separate sets of research questions were formulated for the two lending areas.

With respect to the issue of discrimination in the extension of business loans, six research questions were investigated in this project. These research questions were as follows:

1. Does the approval rate in the award of SBA loans vary between ethnic and racial minority applicants and white (non-Hispanic) applicants?

2. Are there factors other than racial or ethnic bias that explain variation in approval rates in the award of SBA loans to ethnic and racial minority applicants and white (non-Hispanic) applicants?

3. Does the mean loan amount of SBA loans vary between ethnic and racial minority recipients and white (non-Hispanic) recipients?

4. Are there factors other than racial or ethnic bias that explain variation in the mean loan amount of SBA loans to ethnic and racial minority applicants and white (non-Hispanic) applicants?

5. Does the total loan amount of SBA loans vary between ethnic and racial minority recipients and white (non-Hispanic) recipients?

6. Are there factors other than racial or ethnic bias that explain variation in the total loan amount of SBA loans to ethnic and racial minority applicants and white (non-Hispanic) applicants?

With respect to the issue of discrimination in the extension of residential mortgage loans, six research questions were investigated in this project. These research questions were as follows:

7. Does the approval rate in the award of residential mortgage loans vary between ethnic and racial minority applicants and white (non-Hispanic) applicants?

8. Are there factors other than racial or ethnic bias that explain variation in approval rates in the award of residential mortgage loans to ethnic and racial minority applicants and white (non-Hispanic) applicants?

9. Does the mean loan amount of residential mortgage loans vary between ethnic and racial minority recipients and white (non-Hispanic) recipients?

10. Are there factors other than racial or ethnic bias that explain variation in the mean loan amount of residential mortgage loans to ethnic and racial minority applicants and white (non-Hispanic) applicants?

11. Does the total loan amount of residential mortgage loans vary between ethnic and racial minority recipients and white (non-Hispanic) recipients?

12. Are there factors other than racial or ethnic bias that explain variation in the total loan amount of residential mortgage

loans to ethnic and racial minority applicants and white (non-Hispanic) applicants?

The research design for this project provided for the collection of quantitative data directly relevant to the research questions investigated from governmental agencies. These data then were manipulated to reconstitute them in forms that facilitated the assessment of the data with respect to the research questions investigated. Primarily, such manipulation involved the conversion of absolute data to percentages. In other instances, some data sets were combined to cause the data to conform to the operational definition of ethnic and racial minority used in this research.

With respect to discrimination in relation to residential mortgage lending, it was concluded that, while HMDA data and studies based on this data provide evidence of disparities between racial and ethnic groups in the approval of home mortgage loans, such evidence does not support conclusively charges of racial discrimination in home mortgage lending. Nevertheless, as a very minimum, these studies indicate a strong potential for and an appearance of the existence of such discrimination.

Becker's theoretical approach to the issue of discrimination in lending against racial minorities appears to be nothing more than an apology for the practice. Becker appears to ignore the facts of the situation. Babbie's conflict theory has some appeal; however, it does not provide a complete explanation. The view of accommodation within the context of the race relations cycle, while not providing a perfect explanation of the practice, does appear to provide a better explanation than either of the other theories.

With respect to discrimination in business lending, a conclusion was drawn that racial and ethnic bias does explain some of the outcomes of SBA lending practices. Racial and ethnic bias, however, was not the only factor involved in different outcomes. Thus, it can be concluded that the SBA is making an honest effort to improve access to financing for minority group applicants

The findings that the SBA may be making an honest effort in the Los Angeles area to extend business credit in the absence of discriminatory practices, however, must be qualified on two counts. First, the SBA, as an agency of the federal government operating under a Democratic Party president at the head of the sitting administration, may be expected to be more sensitive to racial and ethnic discrimination than are many private sector lenders and than the SBA itself may be under the control of an administration less favorable to minority rights.

Second, the data for the analyzes, the results of which were presented in this chapter, was drawn from the Los Angeles metropolitan area. Lending practices in the Los Angeles metropolitan area reasonably may be expected to be more sensitive to racial and ethnic discrimination that may be true in some other areas of the United States, whether the entity approving or extending loans is either affiliated with the federal government or is in the private sector of the economy.

These two qualifications do not compromise the findings of the research. These two qualifications, however, do serve as a caution against an indiscriminate generalization of the findings reported in this chapter to all lending agencies, regardless of geographic location in the United States, and to all private sector lenders in the country.

CHAPTER 6:
CONCLUSION

For any number of years, allegations of discriminatory practices in the mortgage finance sector have appeared in the press. Wyly, Atia, Foxcroft, Hammel, and Phillips-Watts (2006) stated that predatory home mortgage lending has become a central concern for housing research, public policy, and community activism in American cities. Regulatory attempts to halt abuses have been undermined by claims that "predatory" cannot be defined or distinguished from legitimate subprime lending, and claims that the industry performs a public service via meeting the needs of low-income, high-risk consumers who would otherwise had been denied credit. Wyly, et al (2006) suggest that in recent years most American borrowers have become de facto subprime borrowers because the American system of housing finance has undergone a dramatic restructuring, making mortgage credit more widely available.

At issue in this research is a discussion of whether subprime mortgage lending is in effect a form of discrimination taking place in the mortgage lending sector which specifically targets minorities and lower-income households. Drawing upon various data collected by the Home Mortgage Disclosure Act (HMDA) and its government organ, this report will advance the argument that there is some evidence of disparities between racial and ethnic groups in the approval of home mortgages, but that it is extremely difficult at best to conclusively prove that this has occurred. Further, when one recognizes that *Calculated Risk* (2007), an organization tracking HMDA data on high priced loans, contends that we live in a debt-based economy which makes all borrowers subprime, these disparities may be less significant than is often alleged.

Brooks and Ford (2007, p. A1) have stated that "as America's mortgage markets began unraveling this year, economists seeking explanations pointed to 'subprime' mortgages issued to low income, minority, and urban borrowers. But an analysis of more than 130 million home loans made over the past decade reveals that risky mortgages were made in nearly every corner of the nation, from small towns in the middle of nowhere to inner cities to affluent suburbs." While Brooks and Ford (2007) recognize that subprime mortgages have surged, they also note that these mortgages were initially aimed at lower-income consumers with spotty credit, and that this has in fact changed. Just as subprime lending has increased, high rate mortgages accounted for 29 percent of the total number of home loans originated in 2006, up from 16 percent in 2004. Brooks and Ford (2007, p. A1) further state that "banks and other mortgage lenders have long charged higher rates to borrowers considered high risk, either because of their credit histories or their small down payments." At the same time, these analysts contend that banks have been using subprime rates for middle class consumers seeking to purchase homes with higher price tags than they might normally be permitted to purchase.

HMDA data described by *Calculated Risk* (2007) now includes information on denied applications as well as originated loans and demographic information on all potential borrowers regarding race, sex, and income level. This occurred in 1989 as a consequence of Congressional action based largely on anecdotal evidence that minority and female applicants were being turned down for mortgage loans in disproportionate rates. In addition, in 2002, the Federal Reserved used Congressional authority to augment HMDA reporting requirements to include price data on loans originated because once again, anecdotal evidence suggested that some classes of borrowers were getting higher rates on loans in ways that could not be explained by either the loan or borrower characteristics.

HMDA data does not include FICO – a credit worthiness scale developed in the 1950s by Fair Isaac & Co. – and therefore cannot be used to conclude that higher rates given to lower income or minority borrowers are explained by their subprime credit. In essence, HMDA data is not adequate as it is now constructed to provide a meaningful empirical and statistically sound test of the hypothesis that subprime mortgages are being given only to subprime borrowers or that subprime borrowers with poor credit histories are being given only higher rate mortgages (*Calculated Risk*, 2007).

Reade (2006) has commented that since the 1990s, the strong and rapid growth of the subprime lending sector has changed the mortgage lending industry. Using risk-based pricing, lenders look at the characteristics of potential borrower, estimate the chance of early termination of the loan either through default or prepayment, and thereby determine how to price the loan. Higher risks, said Read (2006), are typically offset by higher interest rates, fees, or both. What the subprime lending sector does is to offer a wide variety of mortgage products to a wide range of households, some of which might not otherwise be able to own a home. Nevertheless, Read (2006) acknowledges, as do others, including Wyly, et al (2006), that despite the fact that the growth of the subprime market played a role in increasing access to credit for traditionally underserved populations, there are persistent concerns that these populations are more likely than others to be overcharged for credit. In addition, and perhaps more troubling is that applicants who qualify for prime, less expensive mortgage products may be steered to subprime products or subprime specialty lenders – a practice that somewhat unexpectedly disproportionately affects minorities (Read, 2006).

Definitively proving, based on HMDA data, that discriminatory practices such as racial steering are at work is a challenging task at best. Bergquist (2006) states that lenders are required to report the spreads on subprime mortgages in addition to denial rates. Because this is the case, it is far easier for analysts looking at the question of discrimination in lending to determine at least superficially, if discrimination has occurred. Bergquist (2006) reported that the Center for Responsible Lending, a nonprofit organization, used a regression model that found glaring racial disparities in the treatment of American mortgage applicants. This study found that Hispanics and African-Americans with the same credit scores than whites tended to receive more expensive loans. A spokesman for this organization told Bergquist (2006) that according to its 50,000 loan survey, Latinos and blacks with similar credit characteristics to whites were more than 30 percent more likely to get a higher cost loan than whites.

Countering this, said Bergquist (2006), are several other bits of information, also taken into consideration by lenders. These data include whether or not the borrower is a first-time homebuyer, a person with a limited work history, and a single household income. Other research reported by Bergquist (2006) highlights the fact that the number of first-lien home purchase loans to African-Americans and Hispanics grew at nearly twice the rate for non-Hispanic whites. The share of first-lien, owner occupied home purchase loans with rate spreads – yields at least three percentage points higher than comparable U.S. Treasury bonds – nearly tripled in 2005 to 15.5 percent. As significantly, Bergquist (2006) states that when considering the subprime market and its target customers, one must also recognize that a number of these loans are for refinancing. What this suggests is that white homeowners and other middle and upper class homeowners have simply chosen to take advantage of lower interest rates to refinance homes that had been purchased at a higher interest rate. Because these individuals have proven their ability to pay, they are ideal candidates for refinancing and this does not make the practice in any way discriminatory.

Nevertheless, the debate over whether or not HMDA data supports the conclusion that there is ongoing and substantial discrimination in mortgage lending that negatively affects minorities is unending. Saul Solorzano (2007), the Executive Director of the Central American Resource Center, spoke before a U.S. House of Representatives Committee and stated that the Department of Housing and Urban Development reported in 2000 that mystery shoppers for loans revealed that nearly one in every five Hispanic buyers and more than one in four Hispanic renters experienced some type of discrimination. In his view, as well as that of other civil right advocacy organizations, the subprime lending sector is a predatory sector that gives little attention to the real needs of minorities for equity in terms of access to affordable home mortgage loans. Swindell (2006) contends that groups such as the NAACP are intensifying lobbying efforts to convince the Congress to pass legislation curbing predatory lending practices for home mortgages.

Various bills are in committee at the present time that address this issue, but Fox (2007) asserts that there is still inadequate evidence supporting the contention that widespread discriminatory lending continues to occur in the United States. Fox (2007) claims that while many people have gotten what turned out to be bad mortgages, many more Americans have been empowered by HMDA changes and have become able to purchase homes.

A surge in subprime mortgage loans to borrowers with poor credit records is ending badly. Fox (2007) cites data suggesting that in today's market, a wave of foreclosures is underway that could at worst cost billions, throw millions of people out of their homes, and cause a nationwide recession. This has happened, said Fox (2007), as a result of several related transitions occurring in the lending sector. First, in the early 1990s, studies were undertaken indicating that minorities were victims of lending discrimination. This brought about changes in lending practices, federal regulations, and HMDA data analysis. Next, Congress passed new legislation aimed at pressuring banks to increase their presence in poor and minority neighborhoods. The result was a sustained and steady increase in home ownership among minorities. For low-income applicants, mortgage denials went from 44.3 percent in 1998 to 19.8 percent in 2003 (Fox, 2007).

Despite this, Swindell (2006b) states that Democrats in Congress expressed the belief that the federal government was not doing enough to help stamp out racial discrimination in the subprime mortgage market. Given that the subprime market had grown to represent 20 percent of the home mortgage market at more than $600 billion, such charges, if true, would be significant. The problem is that the HMDA data does not contain any of the FICO data which is needed if one is going to prove definitively that discrimination is taking place in the mortgage sector.

Another way of looking at the problem was presented by Bergman (2004) who reported that HMDA data presented by race and income does lead to a recognition that in the aggregate, blacks and Latinos are turned down more often than whites for loans, but overall, the number of loans to minorities continues to increase. Denial of a home loan is a traumatic experience, but this does not necessarily mean that it is the result of overt, institutionalized racism. If one includes data regarding income and credit history in analyzing whether or not a potential borrower is credit worthy, race suddenly becomes much less likely to be the primary determinant of eligibility for a loan. Any individual with a spotty work history and a poor history of paying off his or her bills is, quite simply, not a good credit risk.

Part of the problem that is ignored is that predatory lenders who service subprime borrowers may be selling these clients loans that they know cannot be paid off because of the limited income or other financial obligations of the borrower (Wyly, et al, 2006). If this is the case, then what is discriminatory about the practice is not that more at-risk minorities do not get subprime loans, but that so many do get them.

The goal of making home ownership possible for all Americans is certainly an admirable goal. Bergman (2004) has noted that home ownership is integral to the American dream and that denial of a home loan may negatively affect borderline borrowers who might once have worked with a bank to improve their credit to qualify for prime loans. Those borrowers increasingly turned to subprime lenders, in part because the increased use of automated underwriting standards makes it harder for banks to accommodate borderline borrowers. With loans to low-income and moderate income neighborhoods at a 10 year high, Bergman (2004) maintains that the industry needs to do more pre-qualifying counseling of potential borrowers so that they are better prepared to take on the costs of home ownership.

The 2006 HMDA data as described by Avery, Brevoort, and Canner (2007), is limited despite the fact that it now incorporates far more information about successful and unsuccessful mortgage applicants than in the past. This data alone does support the tentative conclusion that blacks and Hispanics were more likely and Asians somewhat less likely to have received higher priced loans than non-Hispanic whites. However, Avery, Brevoort, and Canner (2007) do note that the data collected by HMDA does not account fully for variation in loan pricing across geographies and groups. Loan-to-value (LTV) ratios and measures of borrower credit history are not included in HMDA data. If these essential data which are regularly used by lenders in deciding who will and who will not get a loan and the rate at which the loan will be granted, are not included, then claims of racial discrimination can only remain unproven or at the very most tentatively confirmed. This is not to suggest that discrimination is totally absent in the home mortgage sector. More than anecdotal evidence is needed to either prove or disprove this claim and since such data are available, it seems necessary at this juncture to conduct the type of study that will put this issue to rest once and for all.

REFERENCES

Avery, R.B., Brevoort, K.P., & Canner, G.B. (2007). The 2006 HMDA data. Available at www.federalreserve. gov/pubs/bulletin/2007/pdf/hmda06draft.pdf.

Bergman, H. (2004). Nonwhites getting more loans, but more denials, too. *American Banker*, 169(199), 3.

Bergquist, E. (2006). Pricing studies clash again on racial steering. *American Banker*, 171(106), 18.

Brooks, R. & Ford, C.M. (2007). The United Stats of Subprime. *The Wall Street Journal*, 250(86), A1+.

Fox, J. (2007). Subprime's silver lining. *Time*, 169(14), 53-54.

HMDA data on high price loans. (2007). *Calculated Risk*. Available at http://calculatedrisk.blogspot.com/.

Reade, J. (2006). Home Mortgage Disclosure Act: New pricing data. *News from the Bank*. Available at www. bos.frb.org/ccmmdev/c&b/2006/hmda.pdf.

Solorzano, S. (2007). Home Mortgage Disclosure Act. *FDCH Congressional Testimony*. Available at http://web.ebscohost.com.

Swindell, B. (2006). Report: Minorities often stuck with high-price mortgages. *Congress Daily*, May 31, 6.

Swindell, B. (2006b). Dems criticize racial discrimination in subprime mortgages. *Congress Daily*, June 13, 8.

Wyly, E.K., Atia, M., Foxcroft, H., Hammel, D.J. & Phillips-Watts, K. (2006). American home: Predatory mortgage capital and neighborhood spaces of race and class exploitation in the United States. *Geografiska Annaler,* 88(1), 105-132.

ENDNOTES

[1] A. Edmond, Jr., "Small Business News," *Black Enterprise* 24 (January 1994), 27.

[2] M. Zate, "The Golden State Blues," *Hispanic Business* 16 (June 1994), 24.

[3] J. Saddler, "SBA Vows More Lending For Minorities and Women," *Wall Street Journal* (11 July 1994), B1.

[4] C. Cummins, "SBA's New Head to Focus on Minorities, Needy Areas," *American Banker* 158 (23 September 1993). 3.

[5] M. Mensheha, "SBA Aims to Widen Access to Funding For Minorities, Other Underserved Groups," *American Banker* 159 (25 February 1994), 3.

[6] A. Bianchi, "SBA Loans Spur Start-up Growth," *Inc.* 14 (November 1992), 66.

[7] I. Yokoi, "Korean-, Japanese-Americans Unite Against SBA Loan Measure," *Los Angeles Times* 16 October 1992, B3.

[8] J. Burton, "Razed Hopes—Korean Americans Struggle to Rebuild After Riots," *Far Eastern Economic Review* 155 (1 October 1992), 26-27.

[9] M. Smith, "'I Want to Be the Banks' Worst Nightmare,'" *Business Week* (3 February 1993), 65.

[10] Cummins, 3.

[11] A. Barrett, "Giant Steps For Small Business," *Business Week* (9 May 1994), 53-54.

[12] G. B. Canner, D. S. Smith, N. E. Bowen, F. M. Benkovic, S. A. Freeland, C. H. Johnson, T. A., Orndorff, and M. R. Schultz, "Home Mortgage Disclosure Act: Expanded Data On Residential Lending," *Federal Reserve Bulletin* 77 (1991): 864.

[13] Ibid.

[14] J. Seiberg, "Civil Rights Groups Planning Suits to Spur Minority, Low-Income Loans," *American Banker*, 159 (14 October 1994): 1-2; K. D. Shaw, "Fair Lending Myths," *Bankers Magazine*, 178 (January-February 1995): 4-6.

[15] R. Pear, "A Lending Plan for the Distressed," *New York Times* (Local ed.), 18 January 1993, D1.

[16] S. Cocheo, "CRA: Good Intent Gone Wrong," *ABA Banking Journal*, 87 (April 1995): 9-10.

[17] R. M. Garsson, "Bottleneck in Congress for Two Major Banking Bills," *American Banker*, 159 (21 July 1994): 1-2.

[18] J. Seiberg, "New CRA Rules Get Warm Reception—with Reservations—From All Sides," *American Banker*, 160 (20 April 1995): 1-2.

[19] Smith, 65.

[20] D. Foust, "No Credit Doesn't Necessarily Mean Bad Credit," *Business Week*, 24 June 1992, 43.

[21] A. Srinivasan, "Intervention in Credit Markets and Development Lending," *Economic Review* (Federal Reserve Bank of Atlanta), 79 (May-June 1994): 13-27.

[22] Foust (1992), 43.

[23] Z. Schiller, "Minority Lending: BANC One Gets A Move on," *Business Week*, 14 December 1993, 100.

[24] Canner, et al., 859-881.

[25] M. A. Indick, and T. J. Delaney, "The Community Development Banking Act," *Banking Law Journal*, 112 (January 1995): 4-23.

[26] Canner, et al., 859.

[27] G. S. Becker, "The Evidence Against Banks Doesn't Prove Bias," *Business Week*, 13 April 1993, 13-18.

[28] Indick and Delaney, 4-23.

[29] Ibid.

[30] Ibid.

[31] Canner, et al., 864.

[32] Ibid.

[33] Ibid.

[34] E. Babbie, *The Practice of Social Research*, 6th ed. (Belmont, California: Wadsworth Publishing Company, 1992), 31-34.

[35] Becker, 13-18.

[36] Ibid.

[37] Ibid., 18.

[38] Ibid.

[39] Ibid.

[40] Ibid.

[41] Babbie, 57.

[42] D. Foust, "Taking A Sharper Look at Bank Examiners," *Business Week*, 23 July 1993, 99-100.

[43] Indick and Delaney, 4-23.

[44] Schiller, 100.

[45] Indick and Delaney, 4-23.

[46] Ibid.

[47] Ibid.

[48] Canner, Smith, Bowen, Benkovic, Freeland, Johnson, Orndorff, and Schultz, 1991, p. 864

[49] Ibid.

[50] Ibid.

[51] Ibid.

[52] A. Edmond, Jr. "Small Business News," *Black Enterprise*, 24 (January 1994): 27.

[53] M. Zate, "The Golden State Blues," *Hispanic Business*, 16 (June 1994): 24-25.

[54] J. Saddler, "SBA Vows More Lending for Minorities and Women," *Wall Street Journal*, 11 July 1994, B1.

[55] C. Cummins, "SBA's New Head to Focus on Minorities, Needy Areas," *American Banker*, 158 (23 September 1993): 3.

[56] M. Mensheha, "SBA Aims to Widen Access to Funding for Minorities, Other Underserved Groups," *American Banker*, 159 (25 February 1994): 3.

[57] A. Bianchi, "SBA Loans Spur Start-up Growth," *Inc.* 14 (November 1992): 66.

[58] I. Yokoi, "Korean-, Japanese-Americans Unite Against SBA Loan Measure," *Los Angeles Times*, 16 October 1992, B3.

[59] J. Burton, "Razed Hopes--Korean Americans Struggle to Rebuild After Riots," *Far Eastern Economic Review*, 155 (1 October 1992): 26-27.

[60] Smith, 65.

[61] Cummins, 3.

[62] A. Barrett, "Giant Steps for Small Business," *Business Week*, 9 May 1994, 53-54.

BIBLIOGRAPHY

Babbie, E. *The Practice of Social Research*, 6th ed. Belmont,
California: Wadsworth Publishing Company, 1992.

Barrett, A. "Giant Steps For Small Business."
Business Week (9 May 1994), 53-54.

Becker, G. S. "The Evidence Against Banks Doesn't Prove
Bias." *Business Week*, 13 April 1993, 13-18.

Bianchi, A. "SBA Loans Spur Start-up Growth."
Inc. 14 (November 1992), 66.

Burton, J. "Razed Hopes—Korean Americans Struggle
to Rebuild After Riots." *Far Eastern Economic
Review* 155 (1 October 1992), 26-27.

Canner, G. B., and Smith, D. S. "Expanded HMDA
Data on Residential Lending: One Year Later."
Federal Reserve Bulletin 78 (1992), 801-825.

Canner, G. B., Smith, D. S., Bowen, N. E., Benkovic, F.
M., Freeland, S. A., Johnson, C. H., Orndorff, T.

A., and Schultz, M. R. "Home Mortgage Disclosure
Act: Expanded Data On Residential Lending."
Federal Reserve Bulletin, 77 (1991): 859-881.

Cocheo, S. "CRA: Good Intent Gone Wrong." *ABA
Banking Journal*, 87 (April 1995): 9-10.

Cummins, C. "SBA's New Head to Focus on Minorities, Needy
Areas." *American Banker* 158 (23 September 1993), 3.

Edmond, A. Jr. "Small Business News." *Black
Enterprise* 24 (January 1994), 27.

Foust, D. "No Credit Doesn't Necessarily Mean Bad
Credit." *Business Week*, 24 June 1992, 43.

Foust, D. "Taking A Sharper Look at Bank Examiners."
Business Week, 23 July 1993, 99-100.

Garsson, R. M. "Bottleneck in Congress for Two Major Banking
Bills." *American Banker*, 159 (21 July 1994): 1-2.

Indick, M. A., and Delaney, T. J. "The Community
Development Banking Act." *Banking Law
Journal*, 112 (January 1995): 4-23.

Mensheha, M. "SBA Aims to Widen Access to Funding
For Minorities, Other Underserved Groups."
American Banker 159 (25 February 1994), 3.

Pear, R. "A Lending Plan for the Distressed." *New York
Times* (Local ed.), 18 January 1993, D1.

Saddler, J. "SBA Vows More Lending For Minorities and
     Women." *Wall Street Journal* (11 July 1994), B1.

Schiller, Z. "Minority Lending: BANC One Gets A Move
     on." *Business Week*, 14 December 1993, 100.

Seiberg, J. "Civil Rights Groups Planning Suits to
     Spur Minority, Low-Income Loans." *American
     Banker*, 159 (14 October 1994): 1-2.

Seiberg, J. "New CRA Rules Get Warm Reception—
     with Reservations—From All Sides." *American
     Banker*, 160 (20 April 1995): 1-2.

Shaw, K. D. "Fair Lending Myths." *Bankers Magazine*,
     178 (January-February 1995): 4-6.

Smith, M. "'I Want to Be the Banks' Worst Nightmare.'"
     Business Week (3 February 1993), 65.

Srinivasan, A. "Intervention in Credit Markets and Development
     Lending." *Economic Review* (Federal Reserve Bank
     of Atlanta), 79 (May-June 1994): 13-27.

Yokoi, I. "Korean-, Japanese-Americans Unite Against SBA Loan
     Measure." *Los Angeles Times* 16 October 1992, B3.

Zate, M. "The Golden State Blues." *Hispanic
     Business* 16 (June 1994), 24-25.

www.ingramcontent.com/pod-product-compliance
Lightning Source LLC
Chambersburg PA
CBHW021235280526
45784CB00005B/2111